# Shattered By God's Design

*Lessons of Faith and Hope*

## by
## Cassandra Willis

*Be Blessed*

*Watersprings*
PUBLISHING

*Shattered By God's Design*
published by Watersprings Publishing, a division of
Watersprings Media House, LLC.
P.O. Box 1284
Olive Branch, MS 38654
www.waterspringsmedia.com
Contact publisher for bulk orders and permission requests.

All Bible verses are from the New Living Translation Bible Version

Printed in the United States of America.

Library of Congress Control Number: 2021904234

ISBN-13: 978-1-948877-82-4

# Table of Contents

# Dedication

This book is dedicated to my husband Gary, who has allowed me to tell his story so that others may draw closer to our Lord and Savior and experience what it means to fully surrender to our Father and live a life in Christ. Through it all, your faith has not wavered and your love for God has grown stronger. Thank you, for being my king and a man after God's heart. I can only hope this book makes you proud and showcases the amazing God we serve.

Also, to my children Gary Jr. and Taylor Marie.
You have endured more than most people your age
yet have persevered and triumphed through it all.
Thank you for always loving me even when I could not
always be the mom you needed.
You are both the best gift Jesus ever gave me,
and you will always have my heart. I love you both!

A special dedication to
**Adelaide Hendrix (1943–2020)**
My Beautiful Mother
My faith is because of you
My Love for God is because of you
Everything good in me is because of you,
I love you...I miss you...You are forever in my heart
One day we will read this book together
Under the Tree of Life
Until that day rest my sweet Mother
Lord Jesus come quickly.

# Foreword

On Thursday morning, I received a text. Not just any text, but THE text. "The doctors have told Cassandra to prepare for the worst." My heart sank and to be honest with you, so did my faith.

A few weeks before receiving this text, I led our entire church body in prayer regarding a surgical procedure that Gary Willis was about to undergo. I had also met with Gary and his wife Cassandra at their home. I was confident that the surgery would produce favorable results and Gary would soon have a powerful testimony to share of God's mighty healing power. Unfortunately, this was not the case. Gary's surgery led to unforeseen complications that left us continually interceding to God on his behalf. As the days and weeks passed, Gary's health continued to decline.

The night before I received that dreaded text, we as a church family had just prayed fervently for our church members who were hospitalized or recovering from illness. Gary Willis was once again included in that prayer. At this point, we had done all that we could do within the sphere of our human understanding of faith and prayers. Yet, things were going the other way. So on Thursday morning, upon learning the prognosis of our beloved church member and friend, I asked the Pastoral staff to join me in a visit to the hospital.

When we arrived at the hospital, we saw a large number of individuals who had received the same text message gathered in the waiting room singing, praying, and crying out to God. We joined them in prayer, praise, and worship. We offered comfort to Cassandra and her family as well as encouraged each other in the Lord. We did this believing in the power of God yet facing the harsh, cruel reality and possibility that our prayers would not be answered the way we desired.

When I left the hospital that day, I felt that my presence and prayers were just for support to the family, but there was no way this could turn around. I recall having to leave for a weekend trip to preach for convocation in Sparks, Nevada. It was very difficult to concentrate because I was dealing with the emotions and reality that I left behind.

I steeled myself for the notification that Gary was no longer with us. Whenever my phone vibrated for a call or message, I was nervous to look at it. However, the bad news did not come that weekend, and it did not come in the subsequent weeks. In fact, what played out continuously was the visible demonstration of God's miraculous Hand. Through a series of ups and downs, God brought Gary back from the brink of death before our very eyes, before my very eyes!

This journey was the trying of faith and patience. It came with several bouts of grueling "wait and see" requirements attended by uncertainty, inconsistency, and anxiety. I watched the strain and stress this situation caused the family and sought to minister to them, barely holding on to my own faith, hoping that things would work out.

My personal sense of pastoral inadequacy was eased by the display of a bold and daring faith by Cassandra. Her posts on social media detailing her journey and feelings, her faith-testing, and her confidence in God were just the buffers I needed to reinforce my own weary conviction. It was this that led me to go to the hospital unannounced one day, hoping that I would see Cassandra alone to have a talk.

Sure enough, when I arrived there, she was sitting in the waiting room meditating. As we spoke, I encouraged her to save and compile all her journals of the experience so that others would be blessed and inspired in days to come. This she promised to do, and it is her account that we are about to read.

There is so much about this miraculous journey that I do not know, but I know that the words written, are real and a true reflection of Cassandra's heart. This work of recollection and testimony will challenge your faith and strengthen your conviction that God is real. Brace yourself for the shedding of some tears, but I promise you that it will be worth the cry.

**Pastor Ainsworth Keith Morris**
*Kansas Ave SDA Church, Riverside, CA*

# Introduction

Life can be filled with a roller-coaster of emotions. One moment you can be experiencing your best life and in a blink of an eye things can change and everything in your life as you know it can come crumbling down and shatter into a million pieces. Pieces that you are sure may never be put back together again. That exact thing happened to me on August 11, 2018, as my husband was wheeled into the operating room for serious yet hopeful surgery on his spine. The surgery proved to be anything but routine and after 10 hours of surgery and major bleeding complications, he was placed in his room with encouraging words from the doctors that he was stable, and the worst was behind us. Those words of peace were short-lived and days later we began a tumultuous five-month journey of facing moments where life was hanging in the balance and the possibility of survival was humanly impossible.

*Shattered by God's Design* will take you on a raw and real journey of lessons that were learned while hopeless and in the valley. Each story will stir up many emotions that will pull at your heartstrings and fill you with peace and hope to help you overcome and get through your own storm. After reading each chapter you will have a space to reflect on the scriptures shared and write down your takeaways to assist you in navigating your own personal obstacles

As you finish this book, I can only pray that your life will be filled with the complete belief that even when God seems distant, He is right there waiting to mend your broken heart. Never forget that every journey is for God's glory. There are always blessings, even in brokenness.

# *Psalm 23:4*

Even when I walk
through the darkest valley,[a]
I will not be afraid,
for you are close beside me.
Your rod and your staff
protect and comfort me.

# Aug 15, 2018, 7:24 a.m.

*God brought my husband through a 12-hour surgery. He is responding to our questions and is becoming more alert. Guarantee, I will have more testimonies to share! This is only the beginning...Praising Him in advance!*

CHAPTER 1

# Early Warning Signs

## The Beginning Before the Beginning

I was born and raised in the Seventh Day Adventist Church. My faith in God has always been and still is a mainstay in my life. Yes, I have definitely had periods over the years, where I have allowed myself to be distracted and a bit removed from His presence. But, even in those times, I never doubted that God is the Creator of the Universe and that He is the one and only true living God.

Despite my belief in His power, I have always found one thing perplexing, and that was the thought of God speaking to me. I can recall hearing many preachers, friends, and family members say how they had heard God speak to them over the years. They knew His whisper in their ear – messages of hope, healing, and restoration. I am sad to declare this, but I honestly do not believe that I had heard His voice in my 48 years of life.

Sometimes I felt discouraged when I heard people share their intimate moments with God. I wondered if something was wrong with my hearing? Or did God save His direct words for 'higher level' Christians who had tons of faith and minimal sins, which truly did not include me? In my mind, God had never spoken to me UNTIL.

Around 2016, I felt God tugging on my heart to give Him more of my time. As this constant wooing to get closer to Him continued, I found myself praying more frequently and listening more intently to hear God's voice. After months of closing my eyes and asking God to simply speak to me, it finally happened. I HEARD HIS VOICE. It was clear, it was strong and extremely audible. I was startled as I heard Him say, "Prepare, your life is about to change!"

Now, to be honest, that was not exactly what I was hoping to hear in my first verbal conversation with God. But, with such clearness in His voice, I knew that I needed to immediately begin to put on my armor of God and get ready for a battle. I found it troubling to prepare for war, not knowing what I would be up against or when the foe would strike. That is what true faith is really all about, so prepare I did.

I prayed harder than ever. I studied The Word while pleading with God to give me a glimpse of what was to come, but He never did. He never showed me all the details. However, He did reveal two things about the journey ahead.

The first thing was that what was coming would shake the foundation of my faith. And second, was that it would not be about money, but it would be directly related to health. This revelation brought fear in me that I had never experienced before. And yet, amidst the fear, I felt peace knowing that if my Father cared enough about me to give me warning signs, then He loved me enough to carry me through the dark valley that I would later experience.

I began to prepare spiritually for the attack that I thought would one day touch my body. I questioned if it would be a heart attack, cancer, diabetes, or some other illness. Not knowing what the future held, I just kept doing what I could to prepare myself spiritually, mentally, and physically. Hoping that my preparation would soften the blow that would be coming my way.

I intentionally chose to spend more time with God. My relationship with Him became a priority. Recognizing and hearing His voice became a joy, rather than a surprise. Yes, I was building an intimate relationship again, and it felt wonderful. Preparing for the battle was making me a new person. I was becoming a warrior for Christ, and I was ready to fight whatever God had in store for me.

I cannot say that the warrior in me did not get scared along the way. But there was something going on inside of me that I cannot fully explain. I could hear God's whisper saying, "It's going to be rough, but I got you."

This went on for almost two years. I pleaded with God to "get this show on the road." I thought I was ready to conquer whatever lay ahead of me. In retrospect, I am so thankful that my loving, all-knowing, and compassionate Father held back the winds of turmoil until He knew I had what I needed to make it through.

Two years down the road, I thought I was preparing for my own personal battle with a frightening health diagnosis but, on August 15, 2018, as my husband was wheeled in for surgery on his spine, it became clear that it would not be me fighting for my life. It would be my husband, Gary, the love of my life, my boo, the father of our two children, the amazing man who loves me just as I am. He would be the one that would have to fight the battle and fight for his life. This realization scared me to my core, but in my fear, I had peace that God was with us.

From that day on, we went on a roller-coaster of ups and downs. Due to numerous blood hematomas building up on his spine, he had to endure three emergency surgeries. The final one left him in a coma, placed on a trach, kidney failure, and no feeling or movement from his waist down. The doctors told us, "Gary is the sickest man in the hospital" and to prepare for what they thought would be his final days.

At times, it appeared that my world was collapsing right in front of me and that I would lose my husband of 25 years. And yet, I felt a strength of magnitude proportion. You see, my Father had already geared me up for the battle. In my weakest moments, I found my warrior spirit! God showed up and gave me the strength I needed to make it through the next spiral of events.

It was indeed a tumultuous time for me and our children, Gary Jr., and Taylor. But the one and only true living God who whispers continued to speak to me and guide me in making the essential life and death decisions about Gary's health. The God who whispers gave me the words to speak to our children who could be losing their father. Never had I been in such a dark place, but I was totally consumed with the light of the Father.

I want to open this book by saying that my remarkable journey of faith that you will encounter in these next pages was truly aligned by the Father. Because of God's amazing grace and bountiful mercy and His absolute love for me, He not only prepared me in advance, but He carried me all the way through. Yes, I wish He would have just spoken the words and fixed everything immediately. But then I would have never been able to experience true faith in God, nor would I be able to share this story with you. I am in awe of God's unwavering love for me.

I pray that by the time you finish reading this book of lessons I learned in the valley of the shadow of death, that you, too, will fall in love with our Father again. And ultimately, that my story will allow you to understand that there is victory when you are *Shattered by God's Design*.

# *Aug 20, 2018, 8:43 a.m.*

*Yesterday my husband had to be rushed back into the OR as he had lost all feeling in his legs. After a scan revealed a huge hematoma on his spine, he had to undergo another traumatic surgery. God performed another miracle through the hands of our amazing neurosurgeon Dr. Tashjian. He came out without any complications and back down the road of recovery. It was definitely a setback. Legs not as strong...BUT not strong yet! We serve the almighty God. It will happen! #praisingthroughthetears.*

CHAPTER 2

# God Has the Final Say

H ave you ever had a dream that just really stirred up your emotions and made you wonder if it was just a random thing because you ate too soon before going to bed, or was it clearly a message from God? As we were several weeks into my husband being in ICU in a coma, I struggled with this recurring dream that I had almost nightly. It was so vivid that when I would awaken, it would linger in my thoughts all day until I would fall asleep, and the cycle would continue.

The dream was always exactly the same, with very little deviation in its content. Even the details of what the children and I were wearing were exactly the same. The dream started with me standing on the platform of a church that was very large, but not familiar to me. The room was filled with family, friends, co-workers, and numerous clergy. The kids and I would be standing together on this platform, holding each other up, never saying anything, just looking into the crowd of so many familiar and unfamiliar faces. Never speaking a word, just looking in awe of the number of friends and loved ones that had filled the room.

As the dream continued, more details of the purpose of the gathering became very clear. The casket, flowers, and organ music made it clear that a funeral was to take place, and that funeral was in honor of my husband, Gary. Yet, the most intriguing part of the dream was that Gary was never there. We were in mourning, yet the one we were mourning was never in attendance. Each time the dream disturbed my sleep, the story never changed. People came, we cried, but the casket continued to be empty.

In complete confusion of the meaning of these night terrors, I couldn't help but wonder if God was telling me to prepare for the eventuality that Gary was not going to make it. Or was He letting me know that tears would come and times would get hard, but that casket did not have my husband's name on it? I stayed in a bit of uncertainty, waiting for God to reveal the meaning of this dream and hoping that the dream meant life versus death.

It was not until I was sitting in the hospital one day having worship and praying over Gary that, out of the blue, God gave me a Bible verse. The verse was Psalm 91:7 (NLT), which states, "Though a thousand shall fall at your side, though ten thousand are dying around you, these evils will not touch you." I read that verse over and over again, trying to gain context of how this applied to my life and my situation.

As days went by, and every breath Gary took was a miracle, I continued to read that verse almost daily. Then it all began to make sense. The verse and the dream with the empty casket were both God telling me that Gary would live, and he would not succumb to his very serious health condition.

I felt comforted by my understanding and application of this text, but I still held on to a little bit of doubt. As people began to die all around us, I feared that Gary would be next. Literally, the patients in the rooms to the left and right of Gary died, but that voice I had discovered kept saying, "But it will not come nigh thee." I witnessed families crying as their loved ones were wheeled out to their final resting place. "But it will not come nigh thee." People falling into nurses' arms as they signed the death certificates of their loved ones. "But it will not come nigh thee." Gary laying seemingly lifeless in room 203, in a coma, lungs collapsed, kidneys dead! "But it will not come nigh thee!" Go ahead and gather your family, they said. "But it will not come nigh thee!" That was it! The dream and the verse all began to make sense.

God, in His mercy, revealed to me that although everyone around me was preparing for Gary to be in the casket...DO NOT BELIEVE THEM! I HAVE THE FINAL SAY! Yes, death was all around, and it looked like it was time, but NO! THIS WILL NOT COME NEAR YOU!" Why? BECAUSE I HAVE THE FINAL SAY!

Although God had told me on numerous occasions that Gary was going to make it, my faith had grown weary. I began to believe the inevitable: death was nearing, and our time as husband and wife was coming to a painful end! BUT GOD! When He says NO, it is a NO!

Most of the doctors assigned to my husband, a few nurses, and some friends had already placed Gary in the casket. Still, God had a different plan, and that plan was to heal my husband and bring him back home to his family. When doubt and fear overcame me and doctors said there was nothing more they could do, I found peace in the words of Psalm 27. I leaned on it, knowing that somehow God would restore what the devil was trying to take.

I guess, in many ways, we had our own tomb experience. Just like when many thought they had seen the last of Jesus, He rose again and conquered death. Just like He did for Gary. Tomb robbed again! God is just that amazing! When we think all hope is gone, God does something miraculous and spectacular and simply blows our minds. Look, we do not serve an ordinary God, but a God that is beyond extraordinary and proves it in many ways. Ways that let you know that He is the one and only true God.

Through this entire process, I have learned that God is in control of the day we breathe our last breath, not man. If you are reading this and you are conflicted about what man is telling you to do versus what God is saying, be in conflict no more. Choose the report of the Lord. It is not an easy task as often choosing God is trusting him to do what you cannot see, but He is and will always be the best choice.

What are you struggling with today? What is the devil trying to get you to believe? Whatever it is, completely surrender it to God and ask Him to guide your path. Take the time to slow down and listen to His voice and let him give you the answers to your deepest questions. His report never fails! Just trust in Him. He always has the final word.

# *Scriptures for Reflection*

## Proverbs 3:5-6

"Trust in the LORD with all your heart; do not depend on your own understanding. Seek his will in all you do, and he will show you which path to take."

## Isaiah 26:3-4

"You will keep in perfect peace all who trust in you, all whose thoughts are fixed on you! Trust in the LORD always, for the LORD GOD is the eternal Rock."

# Aug 29, 2018, 2:04 a.m.

*Lord, help me to trust in you. Help me to let go of the guilt I have when I try to just sleep in or step away from this hospital, even for just a moment. Reduce my anxiety so that my fears do not override my faith. Forgive me when I get weak and my mind begins to wonder. Help me not to neglect being a mom when I am trying so hard to just be a good wife for my husband. Increase my faith in you during this time of great uncertainty. I love you, Lord. #praising through the years*

CHAPTER 3

# The Lord Giveth...

They say that God is not a God of confusion, but I will openly say that through this journey, I have questioned that very thought. There were times when I just did not understand His way, and to be quite frank, felt as though the God that I was raised to love really was not real at all. One day, in particular, made me really question God's ways and the direction he was taking Gary's healing.

It was a Saturday, and, as usual, my cousin Kammie got on the bus and traveled from Las Vegas to be at the hospital with Gary so that I could go home and get some rest. I appreciated those moments of peace and was so grateful for her weekly sacrifice. I am still in awe that she would sacrifice her weekends for my peace. Anyway, on this one particular Sabbath, she arrived after I had left the hospital. The medical staff knew her well and briefed her on Gary's condition. They let her know that he was doing better, and they had decided to remove him from the ventilator. Immediately she called me, and I could hear the excitement in her voice as she said, "Cassandra, they are removing the ventilator!" I did not believe her at first and made her repeat herself. I could not believe it. But God had answered my prayer that on this Sabbath day, He would give us a breakthrough. A feeling of release came over me, and I was so excited all I could do was shout over and over again. "Thank you, Jesus! Thank you, Jesus!"

With an urgency to get to the hospital, I hurried the kids and told them to get ready so that we could see this wonderful miracle that God had done. I am not sure they completely understood what was going on, but I do not think it mattered to them. Just to see their mom smile again was all they needed to know that whatever was going on was good.

I remember telling my friend Candi, and she just shouted and praised with me. I texted my pastor, and he shared the news with the church, and the whole church was praising God. It was a high day, and when I finally reached his room, I could not stop the tears from flowing. For the first time in months, I could finally see just his face without any tubes. It was the most beautiful experience. I think I must have sat there for an hour or so simply looking at him and thanking God for yet another miracle.

Unfortunately, within a few hours, my high came crashing down as it became apparent that Gary's breathing had become labored. He started to gasp, and his oxygen level slowly began to drop. I could see the concern on the doctor's face. I remember going in and out of the room, hoping that each time I walked back in, the monitor would show a different story. I did not want to let go of the progress we had made, but as the doctor headed towards me, I knew that we were headed backward.

She informed me that Gary was headed in the wrong direction, and he may need to be put back on the ventilator. I immediately refused; putting him back on the ventilator. I knew that Gary, even though still highly sedated, would be devastated. I asserted that God would take care of him.

Hours went by, and I would not waver from my decision. I kept saying in my head that God was just testing my faith, and any moment He would move, and everything would change. I told our visitors that Gary would be just fine. "Just wait. Everything is just fine." I believed those words with everything that I had, but as the sun began to set, I realized that God was not going to move in the way I had prayed. As the doctor came back to the room, she informed me that either I made the decision to put Gary back on the ventilator or watch him die a slow, painful death. Of course, I chose the former, and once again, we were depending on a machine to keep him alive.

That night I left the hospital crying, heartbroken, and in total confusion. Why would God allow them to take the ventilator out only to have it put back in? Why would He take my kids on this glorious high only to, hours later, break their hearts? As if they had not already been through enough. What kind of God does that? It felt downright cruel and unfair.

For months I pondered this question of why? I know as you read this, you are waiting for me to share this great epiphany of how God revealed to me why this had to happen. But, still to this day, a year later, it is still a mystery. As I write this, I still do not completely understand God's way. I have begged for understanding, but it never came. I turned to the Bible for perspective. Isaiah 55:8-9 says, "My thoughts are nothing like your thoughts," says the Lord. "And my ways are far beyond anything you could imagine."

In my time of confusion, this text ministered to my heart and reminded me that my simple mind cannot understand the complexity of God's actions. In the midst of chaos, He is creating a masterpiece. I realized that when I cannot see or understand, my faith will carry me. With this knowledge, I was able to relax knowing GOD HAS ME!

I learned many lessons in this situation, but most importantly, I learned that when God looks confusing, God is actually behind the scenes working miracles. All my questions of why are still here and may not be answered until I see the Father face to face, but I know that "All things work together for the good of them that 'love the Lord." I accept His plan, and even when I am confused by His actions, I trust His heart. I am beyond grateful for His unwavering protection of our family as we continue to travel this path of trusting God with our whole heart and leaning not to our own understanding, but to His. There is definitely nothing more difficult than choosing to trust God. Trusting God includes having enough faith to believe that every promise that He has provided in the Bible is true even when we cannot see it.

# Scriptures for Reflection

## 1 Corinthians 14:33

"For God is not a God of disorder but of peace,
as in all the meetings of God's Holy people."

## Job 34:10

"Listen to me, you who have understanding.
Everyone knows that God does not sin!
The almighty can do no wrong.

CHAPTER 4

# Remove the Mask

I have never been much of a writer, and I definitely was not one of those who journaled daily. I always found my writing to be mediocre at best and my weakness academically. It was actually one of the reasons I dropped out of my doctorate program in Educational Leadership because I just lacked the confidence to write. But from the beginning of the time we walked into the hospital, I had a journal with me. It was as if my gift for writing came out during my deepest pain, and I wrote daily as part of my way of expressing my sorrow. I not only wrote privately but posted on Facebook, regularly sharing our journey so that family and friends could keep up with us and experience the miraculous things that God was doing in the corner room on the second floor of Kaiser Fontana Hospital.

As time went on and our days at the hospital continued, writing became healing for me and for others who were following our story. Often, I would see or hear from people who would express that my post had encouraged them and had brought them to a closer walk with Christ. They would tell me how they were praying more and getting into the Word more because of my testimony. "Your faith is strong," they would say, or "I admire you for holding on." Coworkers and fellow church members would even make comments such as "Wow, you are such a good wife" and "You have such a strong connection with God." The accolades continued to come, but the more they came, the less I wrote. Yes, I was grateful for how God was using me. Still, deep down inside, I began to question myself. I wondered if I was being honest to those that had now fully immersed themselves in our journey and were using our story as a tool to their own salvation.

Do not get me wrong. Everything I said was true, but in some instances, maybe not the full story. You see, people had become so enamored with the "hallelujah and shouting" moments of my testimony that I did not dare share with them my moments of weakness where I doubted if God was still with me. I intentionally decided not to share the demons that were starting to terrorize me and tempt me to believe that God was not who I believed Him to be.

The pure torture of living up to what people thought of me and what I was really feeling inside was agonizing and mentally exhausting. But I played the game and played it well, I must say. I wore my mask with pride and refused to take it off. It was simply safer that way. Went to work; MASK ON! Entered church; MASK ON! Dinner with friends; MASK ON! Talked to my mom; MASK ON!

It was only at night when I began to remove my makeup and get ready to get in my lonely bed that I let this imaginary mask come off. And then I cried and cried. Tears of torment, of anguish and pain, and fear of the unknown would run down my face. This was my routine, and each night I relaxed enough for a moment to grieve in my pain only to wake up the next morning and start the deceit again!

Over time I could not continue to wear my mask. I wanted to share that I was dying inside. But how could I, in the middle of my story, flip the switch and change the narrative. I was not brave enough to do it, so instead of staying true to the story I had started to tell, I chose to just go silent and stop writing, cold turkey.

This abrupt stop of communication was noticed by many of our friends and family who were waiting to hear what was going on. Texts came to me frequently, asking why I had stopped sharing and posting updates. I know that my silence made some fear that Gary had taken a drastic turn, and I was not ready to open up fully about his condition. Although that was part of the equation, I finally had to admit that I simply was afraid of letting my friends and family down. You see, they had come to know Cassandra as someone who was filled with strength and faith. Someone who smiled constantly and was the one who, in her own brokenness, encouraged others. The one who was, to many, a superwoman. Yet deep down inside, that superwoman was losing her powers.

Yes, this so-called strong "woman of faith" and "good wife" was beaten down to the core and crumbled like an old, rotted tree. She was someone who cried nightly and pleaded daily that God would go ahead and miraculously get her husband up and walking again. The one who was watching her children fall apart and slip into depression. The superwoman who laid awake every night filled with anxiety, not sure how she was going to make it. The superwomen who wore a smile for the sake of others while knowing that deep down inside she was questioning her faith, struggling with feelings of defeat and overwhelming sadness that was stealing her joy.

I wanted to write that this superwoman was starting to not trust God's plan for her life anymore. I mean, didn't He see my pain, my husband's pain? Doesn't He hear my cry? I wanted to tell my followers that I was sick of hospitals, tired of holidays in rehabs, and just tired of life.

So many times, I wanted to share what was really going on in my heart and mind. But how could I? I would not dare taint the picture many had painted in their minds about me. If I shared the doubt, frustration, and anger, I was really feeling, people might no longer believe that I was this great woman of God. If I opened up, even just a bit, I feared that people would see me for who I was and begin to peel back the layers and discover that I was just like them, heartbroken and sad. I could not allow that to happen, so I just stayed silent. MASK STILL ON!

I am sharing this with you because I want to be real and raw in this book and not sugarcoat the pain that will come when following Christ. You see, so often Christian people never show the downside of life. They try to portray a life framed with a white picket fence when, at times, they are surrounded by barbed wire. They want to go around with all the fake smiles and happy greetings when inside, they are wondering if God has abandoned them. We try to mask everything and not be real about how in this Christian walk, we will have pains, trials, anger, even questions.

We carry guilt in our hearts when if we would just open our Bibles, we would find that even our Heavenly Father while suffering on the cross, asked the question many of us ask. "My God, my God, why have you abandoned me?" (Matthew 27:46, NLT) Yes, even Christ, felt as if He were abandoned as he was dying on the cross so that our sins could be forgiven.

I felt the need to share this message as I know there are many Christians who want to scream in frustration or despair but are afraid that if they do, they are demonstrating a lack of faith in God. Well, I am here to plead with you. Stop wearing the mask. Go ahead and cry. Let it all out! Yell, scream, tell a friend, get counseling. Stop trying to present yourself to your friends and family as this untouchable superhero and let the tears flow. Those who love you can handle it, and most of all, God can take it. He is waiting for us to fall into his arms and give him every ounce of our pain. Take the mask off and release yourself to the father. When you do, you will experience a love that only He can give.

After many internal battles, I removed my mask, and I shared everything: the good, the bad, and the downright ugly. I shared my days of plenty and my days of deficiency. The days I cried, and the days I celebrated. I vowed to share the whole truth, knowing that God would always get the glory. I know that every pain, tear, and low moment belongs to God, and He will use it to win others to him.

So, I give you a challenge. I challenge you to release your pain into the atmosphere and let it go. Cry as you have never cried before and just release it all to Him. Not only in private but in public, share your pains, your hurts, your sorrows, and simply allow the sharing of your journey to be a part of your healing. Find peace in knowing that God is using you to glorify His name and bring others closer to a relationship with Him. Hide no more and go ahead, take off that mask and watch God turn your test into a testimony!

# Scriptures for Reflection

## Matthew 11:28

"Then Jesus said, 'come to me, all of you who are weary and carry heavy burdens, and I will give you rest.'"

## Isaiah 41:10

"Don't be afraid, for I am with you. Don't be discouraged for I am your God. I will strengthen you and help you. I will hold you up with my victorious hand."

## Revelation 21:3-4

"I heard a loud shout from the throne, saying, 'Look, God's home is now among his people! He will live with them, and they will be his people. God himself will be with them. He will wipe every tear from their eyes, and there will be no more death or sorrow or crying or pain. All things are gone forever.'"

CHAPTER 5

# When Breathing Isn't Enough!

Have you ever heard people say, "I'm just thankful to be alive" or "Girl, I'm just blessed to be in the land of the living?" I can say that I have heard these familiar phrases on numerous occasions and have probably said them myself. But as I reflected on these past two months, I realized that these words were no longer part of my story. I just did not believe them to be true anymore.

Please do not misunderstand me. I was, and still am, grateful for the oxygen filling my lungs, the beating of my heart, and the blood flowing through my veins. But even with all of that, I would be lying if I did not admit that I WANTED MORE! Waking up every morning and taking in the fresh air was a blessing, but my heart and soul were craving much more beyond just existing. I wanted to thrive, to smile, to laugh again, to socialize.

I thought that I was content with how God was handling our situation. But for some reason, I got stuck in the rut of needing and wanting more. As I spent an hour scrolling through my Facebook page, it hit me. I wanted to live that "Facebook" life. You know that life that is filled with perfect smiles, days at the beach, amazing trips, romantic dinners, kids' accomplishments. Yes, that life. A life that goes beyond the cycle of wake up... work... caretake... sleep. I wanted to move beyond a series of inhales and exhales and truly live.

As you read this, you may become appalled by what I am saying. You may be frustrated with the fact that I was not content with just living and grateful that my husband was still with us. If so, you are not alone, as many others thought the same thing. When I shared with a few people about my feelings, they would reprimand me and say how happy I should be that my husband was alive, that I had a good job, and my health. Yes, I had so much to be grateful for, but I had so much that I had lost, and at that moment, their words brought more pain than comfort.

I constantly battled with being grateful for all God had done and suffered profound loneliness coupled with anger. Truth be told, the devil and his earthly agents were stealing my joy, and I was masking the fact that I was becoming extremely unhappy. I ignored the amazing modern-day miracle that, despite what doctors said, Gary came out of the coma, was becoming more alert each day, and was starting to communicate with us. That his kidneys were finally functioning again, and his daily appointment with the dialysis team was no longer needed.

I permitted feelings of overwhelming loneliness, sadness, and pure jealousy to consume me. I asked myself, "Why did everyone else's life seem to be moving forward while mine had come to a screeching halt?" Alive yes, but surely not living. I am embarrassed to admit I was more concerned about my Facebook storyline being permanently disrupted than I was about seeing the beauty that was all around me.

The constant questions of "Why me? Why us?" frequented my thoughts and consumed most of my days. I questioned how a loving God who knew the beginning to the end would allow us to enter into surgery knowing the tragic outcome that would follow. Coma...respiratory failure...kidney failure...dialysis...blood clots...infections... paralysis...depression .... the list goes on.

During this time of fear and doubt, I began to question God's love for my family and me. I wondered if taking my next breath was more punishment from God than a blessing. Maybe God was punishing me for the bad things I had done. Or maybe this had nothing to do with me at all and everything to do with my husband. Maybe Gary was paying for his unconfessed sins, and because under God we were one, I too was becoming a part of his punishment.

For days I pondered the sins of my life and those of my husband. I tried to recount everything that we could have possibly done that was displeasing to God. I was desperate to prove why this was happening. In my heart, I knew that God was not one to hold grudges against His children. Still, I could not get out of my head that I must have done something wrong and that all of my "grace tickets" had all been redeemed. I was no longer eligible for anything more than what God had already done for me.

The more I pondered this, it seemed as though the devil was screaming at me that we were not worthy of complete healing and that I was not worthy of Christ's love. The devil convinced me that the situation we were in was my fault. Had my sins gone beyond the scope of grace? Did I not pray enough? Did I not study His word enough? Or maybe, just maybe, my faith was smaller than a mustard seed, and who I thought I was as Christian was simply not true, or perhaps this was just where God wanted me to be so that His name would be glorified.

In John 16:33 (NLT), God says," I have told you all this so that you may have peace in me. Here on earth, you will have many trials and sorrows. But take heart, because I have overcome the world." Although these words are very clear, I could not grasp the thought that if God overcame the world, why couldn't He just say the word and get me out of my misery. At that point, I would have taken any glimpse of Him, but yet His silence remained.

As I wrestled with the why of my situation, a friend shared with me James 5:16 (NLT), which says, "Confess your sins to each other and pray for each other so you may be healed." I read it over and over, and the words that came to mind were CONFESS, BE HEALED! CONFESS, BE HEALED! So, confess, I did!

For days I called out to God to forgive me of my sins and those of my husband and to heal him completely. I probably confessed sins from when I was 5 years old to ensure that I covered everything. I pleaded with God to speak to me and reveal to me anything else I needed to leave at His feet so that Gary would be restored. This daily form of repentance appeared to go unnoticed as our situation seemed to stand still. It was in those moments that I almost lost hope of ever having a happy, joyous life. Yes, we were both breathing, but definitely not living.

I am not sure how long my tug-of-war with God went on. One day I was in full surrender and the next day unsure of His presence in my life. I knew that if I kept going down this spiral of doubting God, I would end up in the hands of the enemy. To shift the atmosphere, I began to study with more vigor, and, through divine inklings, God sent me back to the book of Job.

As I read it, I realized that I was in the middle of my own personal

Job experience. I had lost so much, and God was testing me to see how I was going to respond. Would I be like Job and claim, "The Lord gave me what I had, and the Lord has taken it away. Praise the name of the Lord!" or would I take the advice of Job's wife and curse God and die. Although this is hard to say, there were times I wanted to walk away from God and my family, but as the devil tried to knock me down, God continued to be the soft place for me to land. He sent gentle daily reminders that all of my chaos was part of His plan and that He still was on the throne.

After several weeks, I shifted my pity party into a Praise Jam session. I decided to let praise be my weapon! Every time the enemy would tell me that my life was not of value, I would shout out the name of Jesus, and as my cousin always says, "Devil, GO KICK ROCKS!" When jealousy set in, I would look around and begin to call out all the wonderful things God had blessed me with. Eventually, I began to turn the corner and realized that my life was exactly where God wanted it to be.

Daily, I claimed the promise of Deuteronomy 31:6 that He would never leave me nor forsake me. I can honestly say that when He could have just let me go, He held on to me and loved me with an everlasting love. Even in moments of questioning my own belief, His grace and mercy covered me. For that, I am forever grateful.

Listen, I still sometimes long for the "Facebook" life. But more than "the likes" of FB friends, I want the life that God has for me. I have come to grips with the fact that our lives may never return to the way they were. On days when I feel in total despair, I am sure of this one thing... God will PREVAIL! I proclaim Philippians 1:6 (NLT), which says, "And I am certain that God, who began the good work within you, will continue his work until it is finally finished on the day when Christ Jesus returns." This reminds me that through all our ups of downs, God has not left me, and he will continue to keep me always.

Out of this tumultuous time came a renewed passion for Christ that filled me with peace beyond what I could have imagined. I became thirsty for His word and was once again regaining an intimate relationship with Him. Jesus took my sorrows and turned them into pure joy.

As I released myself wholly to Him, my faith increased. I learned to praise Him through every single tear, knowing that every teardrop was part of His PERFECT plan. That every tear shed was part of was a part of His divine purpose. Every triumph and struggle was intended for my good. There are days I still hurt, but I am no longer downtrodden by my situation. I am grateful for the oxygen that fills my lungs, the beating of my heart, and the blood that flows through my veins because I truly know BREATHING is MORE THAN ENOUGH!

I ask you to step back and reflect on your current situation. What is keeping you from experiencing true joy? Is it jealousy about seeing friend's lives thrive while yours seems to languish? Or perhaps it is the relationship that you want but just cannot seem to keep, or is it the promotion that keeps passing you by? Whatever it is, it is time for you to let it go and live the life that God has for you. Free yourself from trying to live a life that is not part of His design. Never forget that what God has for you, is for you, and you alone. So, sit back and relax. Let Him take over, and I guarantee you will truly live your best life. It will be more, much more than merely breathing.

# *Scriptures for Reflection*

## Psalm 27: 13-14

"Yet I am confident I will see the Lord's goodness while I am here in the land of the living. Wait patiently for the Lord. Be brave and courageous. Yes, wait patiently for the Lord."

## Psalm 46:10

"Be still, and know that I am God! I will be honored by every nation. I will be honored throughout the world."

_____

_____

_____

_____

_____

_____

_____

_____

_____

_____

_____

_____

_____

_____

_____

_____

_____

_____

# Sep 1, 2018, 7:50 a.m.

*With so many ups and downs at times, I was afraid to post any progress as I felt that I may have to recant what I said. I am done with that! People need to hear that God is with us and that His power is greater than any doctor!*

*So, with that in mind, I will SHOUT/POST every victory and glimmer of hope BIG or SMALL that God will provide for us. Hilma L. Griffin-Watson, your words touched my heart this morning! So, here we go. Gary is requiring less and less oxygen. His blood is getting better! Lord, I will not be afraid to share every glimmer of hope provided. Everything for Your glory Lord!*

CHAPTER 6

# Pick Me! Pick Me!

T he day started out like any other Sunday. The sun was shining across the beautiful California sky, and I woke up feeling peaceful and hopeful. Despite our circumstances, I felt good inside and ready to start the day. My son had bought tickets for him and his sister to see *The Avengers,* so after we finished our Sunday chores, I dropped them off at the theater. I was free for the next few hours to do whatever I wished. Of course, I did what most ladies do... Shop and Swipe!

I went to one of my favorite stores and did some major damage. It felt wonderful to splurge on myself. Later, I went to a restaurant to grab something to eat. For some reason, I immediately had a feeling of sadness rush over me—; not just a small feeling, but an overwhelming sense of loneliness. I saw couples enter the restaurant, and I realized that once again, I was by myself. No one to dine with, open my door, or just hold my hand. I was familiar with this emotional state, but that day it took over my spirit, and I felt empty. I could not bring myself out of that state. It was a total contradiction to the peace I had felt all morning.

Although my husband was still in the hospital, I was beyond blessed to have had a strong village of family and friends that had never left me through this excruciating ordeal. Always by my side, taking turns so that I was never alone. I knew that at that moment, I could have picked up the phone and, within seconds, had someone help me through this time of sorrow. But even knowing that, I felt more alone than ever and worried if this loneliness overcoming me would ever change. I worried if I would live the rest of my life eating dinners alone and never with a companion to sit at the table and hold my hand, pull out my chair, or simply order for me.

I questioned whether I would ever recover from this and would anything ever return to "normal." Would I ever be able to have my husband take me out on a date, accompany me on a vacation, sit beside me at church, or simply snuggle with me on the couch? As I questioned all of these things, I came to the realization that I was grieving. Not grieving a physical death, but the death of what our lives were prior to my husband's illness.

As the waitress showed me to my seat, tears began to roll down my cheeks. As I sat down on the patio with no one but myself, the emotions of my current situation took over, and I sobbed and sobbed. Right there on the patio, I began to cry out to God, pleading for Him to help me. I begged, "Lord, please take away this pain, remove this loneliness, remove this doubt."

I expressed to Him how tired I was and how I just wanted one day of peace and relaxation. That I was drained from being a "single" parent and trying to nurture kids who were broken and questioning their own faith. I pleaded for Him to fill my heart with peace, but as much as I wanted to stop crying, I just could not. I did not care who was looking at me and what they may have thought. All I knew was that I needed the Comforter to come and make me whole again, and if that meant a full breakdown on a patio of a public restaurant, then that is what needed to happen.

After many minutes of nonstop tears and several gestures to the waitress to give me a moment, I finally regained my composure and ordered some food. During my meal, I reflected on what had just happened. I began to realize that God had orchestrated this entire moment. He had placed me in this time, in this space, so that He could speak to me without distraction. I knew that the Father was pleading with me to come to Him and cast my burdens at his feet.

I fought against following my normal routine of reaching out to my earthly support group and, in a calm voice, asked my Creator and Sustainer to speak to me. Sitting still at my table with people around me, I closed my eyes. It was then that I heard God saying, "PICK ME!" Remember Me? The Creator of the universe, "PICK ME!" The One who has carried you through it all. "PICK...ME!" The One who took your husband out of a death chamber and brought him back to life. "PICK ME!" The One who has provided and kept you, understands your pain, feels your emptiness, and loves you more than anyone ever will—the One who has felt the same pain of abandonment and loneliness.

As those words repeated in my mind and resonated in my soul, I boldly spoke loudly and unashamedly, "Lord, I pick you!" I said it again and again, "Lord, I pick you!" It was as if I had just freed myself of all these bottled-up emotions, and each time I said that simple phrase, I could feel the presence of the Holy Spirit filling my soul. I knew he had heard me and was reminding me to just "Be still and know that I am God!" (Psalms 46:10, NLT).

I remember smiling and looking towards heaven, knowing that our Father, Jehovah Shiloh, had heard me and was giving me peace. The tears ceased, and I heard God clearly say to me, "Everything is going to be alright." Our precious daughter, who was falling apart mentally, was going to be ok. My husband would walk, my son would overcome his depression, our family would be restored, and I would make it through this. He reassured me that He was my father and He loved me. He would fill the gap in my lonely heart if only I would pick Him.

From that day, I committed to trying God first to depending on Him, and trusting Him first! Ultimately, I have to believe that I cannot see, He can! I encourage everyone reading this to make God your true BFF and use your lonely times to listen to our Father and let Him pour life into your soul. He has a desire to be our closest friend, and more than anything, He wants us to pick Him first.

This was not an easy task, but since that day, I knew that God was taking a new role in my life and had captured my soul once again. I dare you to allow Jesus to be your best friend and confidant. I guarantee He will be the best companion you will ever have or need. He will walk with you, hold your hand, and wipe away your tears. Whatever you need, HE IS! Allow Him to be the lover of your soul. I promise you will never be disappointed again.

# *Scriptures for Reflection*

## 1 Samuel 3:10

"And the Lord came and called as before,
'Samuel! Samuel!' And Samuel replied,
'Speak, your servant is listening.'"

## John 5:25

"And I assure you that the time is coming, indeed it's
here now, when the dead will hear my voice-the voice
of the Son of God. And those who listen will live."

# October 18, 2018, 4:37 a.m.

*Weekly update: Let me start off by saying we serve an amazing God. Now, Gary is progressing. After 61 days, he was finally downgraded from ICU! Yes, glory be to God! Maybe even by next week, he can head to a rehabilitation center to start regaining his strength and mobility.*

*This is nothing short of a miracle! There are still some health issues that we need Gary to overcome. One has to do with his breathing and his blood levels. Without going into details, I ask that you all pray in unity with me that he can pass this test today and his blood will stabilize! I also ask for prayer for God to help me to be able to get him into the best rehabilitation center there is.*

*I am nervous about the two options I have and need guidance. More than anything, please pray for Gary's spirits. He needs the will to fight through this, and right now, he just does not have it. He is physically and emotionally drained. He has been through a lot, but when we talk, his faith in our Lord is strong.*

*If you can and have time, send me a video message of encouragement, and I will play it for him. Encouraging and funny memories would be great! You can message it to me or email me at parentsasheroes@gmail.com. He would be energized to know how many people have been praying and thinking about him. Keep praying! God is not done yet!*

CHAPTER 7

# Simply Just Good!

There I sat in church, unfocused, feeling unclear and uncertain. My body was physically there, but my mind and my heart were definitely far away from this sacred place of worship. Truth be told, if it were not for my kids, I would not have come. But the guilt of not having them attend church overwhelmed me this particular Sabbath. So, I pushed through the desire to stay in bed and forced myself to get up and go to church and fellowship with other believers. I had hopes that it would help me get out of this spirit of doubt that was starting to consume my mind.

As I sat in our Bible study class, I found myself completely disengaged with the word being taught and more focused on the clock. I thought to myself, only two more hours, and this "church experience" would be all over. I could just go home and wallow in my disappointment.

As the service transitioned from Bible study class, I fixed my face and entered the sanctuary with my painted-on smile. I greeted everyone in my path, hoping that the dreaded question of how my husband was doing would not come. I almost made it to my seat without anyone asking. But before I could sit down, it was as if a spotlight was on me. Everyone surrounded me and asked the very questions that I really did not want to answer that day or any day for that fact.

One after another, I engaged each person with a smile responding with phrases such as, "He's fine. Thank you for asking." "Oh, he is great!" "Just awesome!" Exhausted from so many questions, I found myself ignoring others heading my way. I just wanted to find a seat in the corner of the back of the church where few people could see me.

To many, this is a simple question to answer, but for me, it was a constant reminder of the current situation we were in. I felt as if every time that question was asked, I lied not only to the one asking but also to myself. Yes, lie. You see, the truth is that every time I was asked how things were, I found myself fighting not to yell at the top of my lungs, "No, he's not doing fine! Our lives are spinning out of control, and our hopes and dreams are gone."

I wanted to tell them the truth! I wanted to let them know that my husband was weak, that he was in excruciating pain, and cried himself to sleep every night. I wanted to say that he was struggling with depression and discouragement. Should I dare share that I feel hopeless? That's exactly what I wanted to say, but telling the naked truth does not always go over well in the church. So, I chose to play it safe. I kept up the façade that all was well.

As the praise and worship began, I convinced myself I would get through this. I suppressed the tears, regained my composure, and prayed that something in the service would rejuvenate me. I really felt like God had abandoned me. I mean, I had prayed, studied, and trusted God with my whole heart or, at least I had tried to. I stood still, and I believed. I trusted in the words He had spoken to me in various dreams. I heard His voice multiple times telling me clearly that everything was going to be all right, yet in that very moment, I wondered if He had forgotten what He had promised.

Although I was in church sitting in silence, my mind was crying out, "Lord, help me understand! Why am I missing the mark? Why so many ups and downs? Seriously, I cannot take much more! I surrender... I wave the flag...I am done! I wanted the life that I often complained about and had not appreciated, BACK NOW!

As the morning prayer began, I let my thoughts wander even further away from the Spirit that was filling the church. My mind was moving swiftly back and forth between the goodness of God and the wandering of why He would give me dreams of hope and not act upon them. I started to think that maybe I was being let down because I was praying with too much expectation and asking for things that were just too big.

As the prayer continued, I decided I would simplify my prayers. I would just ask for little things with absolutely no expectation. *Yes! That is what I will do. Isn't it better to not expect anything? No expectation means no confusion, no letdowns, no pain, no doubt. I am still believing, just not expecting.* As I got off my knees, I was pleased with my decision to move forward with this mindset. I was at peace and ready to "Get my praise on!"

Fast forward 10 minutes later...Hold up! What did I just say? Did I just say that I would not expect anything from God, the Creator of the universe? The God who took my husband out of a deathbed and rose him up? The God who took dead kidneys and sprung them into life at the last moment before doctors put in a permanent stent. The God who the doctors said was the sickest man in the hospital to be living today! Expect nothing from THAT GOD! Just thinking about it made me want to slap myself. I had seen firsthand that SAME GOD work a modern-day miracle in the life of my husband, and yet I doubted Him. At that moment, I realized that I needed to continue to go boldly before the throne of grace and petition the Father. He has promised to answer our prayers according to His riches and glory (Philippians 4:19, NLT).

The Bible says in Matthew 7:11, "So if you sinful people know how to give good gifts to your children, how much more will your heavenly Father give good gifts to those who ask him." Romans 8:28 says, "And we know that God causes everything to work together for the good of those who love God and are called according to his purpose for them." Two different verses but one keyword in common, and that word is GOOD.

God wants and desires to give us GOOD things. If I trust and believe these words, I must believe that what I had been praying and longing for were, in God's eyes, simply not good for me. Not good now. Not good yet. Maybe, not good ever.

Although this was very difficult to swallow, I knew I must put my faith in Him and cling to Ephesians 3:20 (NLT), which says, "Now all glory to God, who is able, through his mighty power at work within us, to accomplish infinitely more than we might ask or think." Knowing that God could do exceedingly more than I could think was all I needed to push forward and continue this journey with Christ on my side. So back on my knees, I prayed with a new fervor, with greater expectation, knowing that whatever God had for me was good! Not great, but Good!

Today, I choose to live by revelation and not by the situation. I choose to trust His plan for our lives. Is there something that has you tossing in your sleep at night? A part of your life that you just do not understand, and you are confused by how God has responded? You are not alone.

Know that every perfect and good gift comes from God. His love for us is more than we could have ever imagined and everything that He gives us or allows us to go through is good for us. God does not make mistakes, and everything will work out. Hold on, "good" is on the way.

# *Scriptures for Reflection*

## Psalm 31:14-15
"But I am trusting, O Lord, saying, 'You are my God.' My future is in your hands. Rescue me from those who hunt me down relentlessly."

## Hebrews 3:14
"For if we are faithful to the end, trusting God just as firmly as when we first believed, we will share in all that belongs to Christ."

# *September 4, 2018, 5:45 a.m.*

Exactly 21 days ago, at exactly this time, we checked into the hospital for surgery. Our plan was to be in the hospital for a week, then off to rehab... maybe home. Our biggest fear was if Gary would be paralyzed after the surgery.

Well, God had a different plan. His plan would stretch our faith, test if we truly believed Him, make us hit rock bottom, and force me to make life or death decisions. Never felt this much pain in my life. Never been so beat up by the devil. BUT GOD!

At my lowest points, our Lord and Savior came to my rescue. Gave me the strength to keep fighting. To remove my doubt and praise Him through my tears. To help my babies work through their own pain of maybe never seeing their dad alive again!

Every prayer given during my lowest of times, God has answered. When I could not pray, God sent people to pray for me and uplift me. With that, I PRAISE HIM!

Yes, my husband is still in critical condition but guess what HE IS ALIVE! He gets better every day. Doctors were blown away as some of them felt it was over. Listen!!! I do not know how this story will end. I have no idea what God has planned, but this I do know... God has Gary and our family in the palm of His hands. Am I scared? Yes. Are the kids scared? Yes, but we have this hope in the Lord that He is in control! Thank you for your prayers.

#praisinghimthroughthetears

# *September 11, 2018 at 5:00 p.m.*

*We are at 4 weeks now. Words cannot express the joys and pains this situation has brought our entire family. As I sit here next to my husband, my heart is beyond heavy as I know he needs a miracle.*
*I try with everything I have to not allow certain thoughts to enter my mind but keeping it real! I am so tired. I am so broken. The love of my life is lying here, and I feel beyond helpless. I am not ready to say goodbye. I am not ready to have that conversation with my kids...NOT READY!*

*This journey has been one that has ripped me to the core, but I am still hopeful. I am still believing that this situation is bringing someone closer to Christ. Lord, please hear the cries of your daughter. Please help me to stand strong and not give up. Please help me to be encouraged!*

*You are GOD! Save my husband, I pray. Not my will, but Thine will be done. I need everyone reading this to pray fervently for him right now. The tube needs to come out! Lungs need to be cleared! We believe a miracle will be performed. I have seen it done, and I will not give up now. Continue to pray for his mom and siblings as this is just as hard on them as it is on me.*

*#praisingthroughthetears — with Gary Willis.*

CHAPTER 8

# Faith and Finances

Although I would never verbally express my thoughts about some of my parents' decisions, I surely did, at times, second guess them. Do not get me wrong, they were great parents and provided well for us, but every time I saw them put hundreds of dollars into the offering plate, I questioned their sanity. I mean five kids in church school, a mortgage, bills to pay, and let's not forget about summer vacations, Christmas presents, and birthdays.

I often thought who in their right mind would give so much to a church that appeared to be giving nothing in return. I remember asking my parents why they were so, in my mind, "irresponsible" with their money and, their response was always the same, "God will provide." They expressed that God would always supply our needs if we returned a faithful tithe and offering. I must admit that I was extremely skeptical about this, but my parents never wavered from this belief and made sure we knew and understood the practice of giving back to God.

Proverbs 22:6 (NLT) reads, "Direct your children onto the right path, and when they are older, they will not leave it." I never really paid attention to this verse growing up. But I realized 40 years later, the training my parents gave me would become my guidance as my faith and finances collided, and I wondered if we would lose everything.

After weeks and weeks of watching Gary's still, and most of the time, lifeless body lay in his hospital bed, I began to worry as it was evident that this battle was not going to be over as quick as we hoped. The dreams of Gary returning in six weeks had now been shifted to months, maybe even years, if ever.

As this reality set in my mind filled with so many "what if" scenarios, which mostly focused on our finances. What if God did not allow him to live, and his income would be lost? What if I could not pay all of our bills? What if I did not have enough money to pay for my son's tuition or get him into a college? What if I had to pay even a portion of these hospital bills? What if my salary was decreased because I missed so many days?

I had so many questions that I felt as if my faith was no longer present. Worry became a part of almost every moment of my day. Although early on in this journey, God had already given me insight that my finances would not be my major obstacle, in the midst of my bleak circumstance, I allowed what I could not see to blind me to what God was already working out.

As these "what if's" consumed every part of my being, God sent an angel by the name of Steve Coute to give me a little peace of mind. I did not know Steve very well, but I knew my husband thought very highly of him. Having heard of the possibility of Gary not surviving, he called to tell me information that would bring me a layer of tranquility that I needed at that moment.

He informed me that Gary had a conversation with him before the surgery and gave him all of our insurance policies that we had paid into. He explained that if something were to happen to Gary, he wanted Steve to make sure our family was taken care of and had all the information he needed to do so. Steve and I both knew Gary was hanging in the balance between life and death. Although my heart was broken at the thought of losing my husband, in some ways, the news about the policies allowed me to let my guard down just a tiny bit. Money no longer needed to be my focus as my husband had once again done what he always did and took care of our family.

As time moved on, miracle after miracle began to happen. Gary began to come out of the coma, and one by one, tubes and wires were taken out of his body. It became evident that my husband was a survivor and that the worst was behind us. But it was in those moments of joy and happiness that the devil pursued me and began to make me question my faith and finances once again.

The Bible makes it very clear that the devil is active in trying to tempt us to go against the words of our Father and encourage us to lose hope. 1 Corinthians 10:13 states, "The temptations in your life are no different from what others experience. And God is faithful. He will not allow the temptation to be more than you can stand. When you are tempted, he will show you a way out so that you can endure." This text reminded me that I would not be the first person to worry about finances, but would I be one of the ones who would accept His way of escape or fall prey to doubt?

I knew how to get by financially if he would pass, but I did not know how we would survive if he lived. Let that sink in. All my financial woes in his death seemed to be covered, but in life, they seemed to be even more magnified. How would I pay for his medical expenses? How would we redo our home to make it more accessible? How would I pay for a caregiver? How would I get him to his doctor's appointments without a wheelchair-accessible van? Thousands of extra dollars in healthcare expenses every month. How would we survive this? I had found financial peace in death, but thoughts of financial chaos in life.

The stress of finances made me begin to question the values my parents had taught me in regard to returning a faithful tithe and offering and our commitment as a couple to help those in need. I remember thinking, if "God owns a cattle on a thousand hills," what does He need my money for? I began to consider paying just a portion of my tithes and holding money back for Gary's expenses. That would technically be helping someone. I even rationalized the thought that God wanted my son in a Christian school, so taking money for that surely had to be a good use of "God's money."

I admit that I was torn, but every time I considered keeping a bit of money to myself, I would hear my parent's message, "God will provide. God will provide." I knew that one of the guiding principles of our marriage was helping others in need and returning a faithful tithe and offering. As tempted as I was, I could not allow my fears to overcome what I knew in my heart my Heavenly Father could do.

Every month I struggled with helping the charities that were dear to our hearts and giving back to God what was rightfully his. We were living check to check, and that was definitely not in my comfort zone. A turning point came one day as I was listening to a preacher online. He said, "True faith is giving in your own area of need." That resonated with me. Although our financial situation looked grim, I knew I had to exercise my faith and give into the area that I was lacking in the most. Money.

Every time I gave, I felt a sense of joy knowing that God would take my little donations and make them more than what I could ever have imagined. Was it easy? No. Was I tempted along the way? Yes!

There were times of fear and doubt, but I chose to open the box that I had put God in and trusted Him to do beyond what I could see. I claimed God's promise in Ephesians 3:20, and I cannot tell you how many times God did exceedingly and abundantly all that I could ask. These blessings were so overwhelming that I will close with a shortlist of what God has done and is still doing in our lives.

- Millions of dollars of hospital bills – zero co-payment.
- Hotel bill for nights to stay close to Gary completely paid for.
- Went to try and pay my son's bill for school. They told me, "You only owe 50.00. The rest has been taken care of.
- Biweekly gifts of gas cards and food so that our transportation was paid for, and we always had food to eat.
- Went to my cabinet feeling financially overwhelmed and found an envelope my sister had left for me with $1,000 to help out.
- Go Fund me account started by family raised enough money to cover the standing frame that my husband needed.
- Went to the mailbox on numerous occasions finding thousands of dollars in random gifts from people I barely knew just saying they wanted to help.
- The food train that was set up so that we would have meals every day.
- Long term disability plan that I did not know existed began to assist us.
- Mortgage paid on time every month and bills paid.

I can honestly say that when praise goes up, blessings rain down. I am still in awe of what God has done and how He has taken care of us, and how He has given us so much more than what we had before the journey began. Little truly does become much when we place it in our Master's hand. I challenge each of you reading this to trust God. He will prove to you time and time again that He will provide in ways that you could never have imagined. Faith + Finances = Abundant Blessing.

# *Scriptures for Reflection*

## Philippians 4:19

"And this same God who takes care of me will supply
all your needs from his glorious riches,
which have been given to us in Christ Jesus."

## Malachi 3:10

"Bring all the tithes into the storehouse so there will
be enough food in my Temple. If you do, 'says the Lord
of Heaven's Armies,' I will open the windows of heaven
for you. I will pour out a blessing so great
you will not have room enough to take it in!
Try it! Put me to the test!

## Matthew 6:11

"Give us today the food we need."

## Proverbs 22:6

"Direct your children onto the right path,
and when they are older, they will not leave it."

# Oct 26, 2018, 7:34 p.m.

*Gary Willis quotes, "I'm a survivor," and "I'm determined to get better." Love my husband! Faith over fear!*

# Nov 16, 2018, 10:47 p.m.

*So, today I had an Israelite moment. The past few days, I have been filled with anxiety and, truth be told, doubt. Doubting if Gary will be home soon, fearful he will not walk, nervous that I would not be able to take care of him. I was just like the Israelites who saw God's miracles numerous times, but when things were uncertain, they lost hope.*

*Yep, today, I was truly an Israelite. I know God is looking down saying, "Seriously, have you not witnessed a miracle right before your eyes?" This picture says it all! I hear you, Lord BUT I DON'T SEE! Yes, I know that faith is the substance of things hoped for and the evidence of things unseen! I GET IT! But why is it so hard! All I can say is this journey of faith is simply that. One that will make you question a lot, but as I go to bed, I am excited to believe that everything I am fearful of, God will restore. Claiming His promises. Praying for peace. Gary and I both need it.*

# Dec 1, 2018 5:51 a.m.

*To all my God-fearing bible followers; is it ok to ask God why? To feel totally depleted in this journey of faith? To just wonder when it will ever end? Just need some advice today because I am a bit confused. I am sure my FB friends can give me some good words or scriptures. Just need some encouragement and clarity.*
*#stillpraisingthroughthetears*

# June 26, 2019, 1:26 a.m.

Today is a special day. Today my husband and I celebrate our 25th wedding anniversary! It is beyond miraculous that we are able to see this day...BUT GOD!

Today I want to celebrate with my husband. He is truly the strongest man I know. He has fought against death and continues to fight daily to get through the pain he is in while still trying with all he can to guide our family and keep us close to Christ. He is truly my GOAT! My best friend!

Our marriage has had many trials. Not just this year, but years in the past. Trials that have made us both, I am sure, wanting to just walk away, but here we stand. Stronger than ever. Not giving up but working together to get through this current obstacle. Our faith has increased, and our love has grown. We have truly beaten the odds!

It has not been easy, but WE CHOSE FOREVER! Thank you, Babe, for these 25 years. With all our ups and downs, I would not change it for the world! Well, I would change a few things, but you get what I am saying... I love you! Keep pushing...God's not done yet!

CHAPTER 9

# For Better or For Worse...
## Really God?

Entering the hospital, I saw one of my favorite nurses was working the day shift and was assigned to my husband. Having nurses with who I had built a trusting relationship with gave me peace knowing that Gary would be well taken care of. "D," as I affectionately called her, had a sweet spirit that radiated the love of Jesus Christ. Although we had never spoken about God, on one of my tough days, she got on the floor and wept and prayed with me. What I suspected was true. She was a Christian and truly an angel from God.

After our moment of weeping, "D" and I became very close and talked frequently. One day our conversation turned to the subject of marriage. She told me that she and some of the other nurses had been discussing how impressed they were with my dedication to being at the hospital and my commitment to hanging on and not walking away from the situation. She told me that many of them said they did not think their relationship was strong enough to pass the test of for *better or for worse* and that they would most likely walk away. I kind of chuckled at what she said and went about my business.

Although brief, the conversation stayed with me for the rest of the day. I wondered how people who vowed to forsake all others and cling to their spouses, as the Bible commands, could decide to walk away when things got rough. I thought, "Seriously, don't they remember the vows they took before God and their witnesses. For better or for worse...for richer or for poorer. In sickness and in health." This whole conversation was funny yet troubling for me.

The more I thought about it, the more I began to think highly of myself. I began to think, "Yes. Look at me. I am the perfect picture of what a wife should be." Silly as it was, that conversation made me a little haughty, and each day I came to the hospital, I made sure everyone saw me, the wife of the year. Not only did the nurses sing my praises, but over the past year, many women of faith praised me too. "Girl, you are such a strong wife."

At times, I doubted their words, but as the accolades built, I began to wear my badge of "wife of the year" with pride. I held myself in the highest of esteem, looking down on those I knew had chosen to give up on their marriages. "How dare they. Look at me. Follow me. I got this!" Or so I thought I was acting as if I was a martyr for marriage and the poster child for what it meant to stand by your man.

Of course, over time, my crown had less sparkle and was constantly tilted. My sash was tattered and falling to the ground. Any thoughts that I would receive an award for "Wife of the Decade" surely had been destroyed. In all seriousness, it was not because people had changed their thoughts of me, but more so because of the thoughts that I had of myself, my family, and my marriage.

Truth was, throughout this journey, I had come extremely close to packing my bags and simply walking away. Move to another state and simply start over with my kids? *Maybe.* I loved everyone, but I was tired of being tired. The human part of me simply did not want to live this life of taking care of someone constantly and having someone be totally dependent on me for most of their needs. There were things I just did not want to do and, in some cases, did not really know how to do. I was lost between trying to do all that I could to help him with all his needs yet lost in my own inadequacy.

I would go from sad to angry on most days, and more and more, I longed for a different life. I wanted to get up and go to dinner without four transfers into the car that killed my back. I wanted to dance on the floor with my 6' 4" husband holding me. I wanted to take a family vacation without being the one who had to pack everything and drive everywhere. I wanted intimacy again. I WANTED OUT!

I know this does not sound like the "Wife of the Year" who had been introduced at the beginning of this chapter, but it is important that I share with you the good and bad about my journey of faith. I know someone reading this book is struggling to remain in their marriage. You are tired and questioning how much more you can take and are feeling alone. But I am here to tell you that you are not alone.

I have felt like walking away too. To just break free and leave it all behind. I know it is hard. I know you have cried so many tears. I know your heart is broken, and your fairy tale ending has turned into a nightmare. But I am begging you to hold on. Stop trying to heal your own pain. Step back and let God step in and restore. Let Him mend not only your broken heart but also the heart of your spouse. He can do the impossible and reclaim what the devil is trying to destroy.

Say this prayer with me. "Lord, I thank you for being a God of restoration. I ask now that you take away any doubt I have about your sovereignty. Help me to trust you in all things. Lord save my marriage and bring healing to our home. Help us to follow your plan for our lives and give us the tools to keep our marriage whole. Lord, we surrender fully to you. Forgive me of my sins. I give my life to you, father. Have your way in every aspect of my life. Amen!

The main reason I am still here is my love for my husband of 25 years, but more importantly, my love for God. You see, I made a vow before God that I would love and cherish this man "till death do us part." TIL DEATH DO US PART! That was not a commitment that provided provisions for me to escape when things got tough. It was a forever commitment, and because of that, I am still here fighting this battle alongside my husband.

There are days I want to yell, throw things, leave, and never come back, but on those days, I fall on my knees and ask God to give me the strength to rise above the current moment and hold on to the promises that he has given me. Staying in this marriage does not make me a better person or any more special than the lady next to me. All I am doing is following what God has instructed us about marriage: To hold on and allow God to be the glue that keeps it together.

So once again, I say HOLD ON! The enemy is doing everything he can to destroy the family structure. He knows that his time is coming to an end, and if he can destroy the marriage, he often takes the children. Do not give up! Please give this over to the Lord and let Him guide you. He has saved me and changed my heart, and I know He can do the same for you.

# *Scriptures for Reflection*

## Genesis 2:24

"This explains why a man leaves his father and mother and is joined to his wife, and the two are united into one."

## Mark 10:9

"Let no one split apart what God has joined together."

CHAPTER 10

# The Lion's Roar

After three months in the hospital and two months at a rehabilitation center, Gary was mentally ready to come home. I cannot say that he was physically ready to leave the hospital or that our home was ready to support his new life as a paraplegic, but nevertheless, we moved forward with the plan to transition him home. It had been five long months, and his intense desire to be home, coupled with severe depression, made it easy for us to switch the focus from his physical health to his mental health and support his decision to come home. Although I was not ready to become a caregiver, I knew home would be a better place for him to build the mental strength needed for the intense therapy that would be needed in the months, possibly years ahead.

I will never forget his homecoming. Many friends gathered in front of our home with signs and noisemakers as this was a celebration of magnitude proportion. As the transport service pulled up to the house and my son wheeled him out of the van, there was a roar of applause filled with cheers and shouts of praise. I could barely contain myself as the tears rolled down my face, and I fell into his arms. Together, we thanked God for all the great things He had done.

Over the next few months, we began to adjust to our new life at home. I learned how to do transfers into the bed and to do all the intimate details of taking care of someone immobile. It was truly the hardest thing I had ever done in my life. The daily lifting and the demands of running the household and taking care of the kids while sleeping less each day were definitely taking their toll. I felt excited and relieved when I was informed that Gary qualified for another round of inpatient therapy. It was not as if I did not want him home, it was more the fact that I simply needed a break, and if that break included Gary getting more thera-py, then that was a double blessing. Together we prayed that God's will would be done and if leaving home for a bit was the best thing for us as a family that he would open the doors and open the doors he did.

Two weeks into his stay, we could see a noticeable difference in not only his physical strength but also his speech. Gary's legs were loos-ening up, and he was able to stand more and attempt to take steps. His body was getting stronger, and I just knew he would be walking before he left the hospital.

We were on a great path. I was starting to believe that our life was going to make a shift, Gary would be walking soon, and things would be back to "normal." But even in the midst of all the excitement, I noticed something was off with Gary. Usually, we would talk 2-3 times per day, but our time on the phone was slowing down to maybe one time per day.

Although it was strange, I had so much on my plate with work and the kids I did not make a big deal about it and pushed it to the back of my mind. I did not become nervous until our phone conversations became minimal and consisted of one-word answers or short phrases. On some occasions, I would ask him questions, and he would simply not respond. The more I called, the less he answered, and fear began to creep in. I questioned the hospital staff about this new behavior, but they stated that he was fine. But when you have been with someone for over 25 years, you know when something is just not right. Soon I would realize that my suspicions were correct, and we were dealing with a dif-ferent type of illness that we had never experienced before.

It was a Wednesday when I received a call from Gary's nurse saying that he was acting quite unusual and incoherent. Immediately I jumped in my car and raced to the hospital, unsure of what I would find. During the entire 45-minute drive to the hospital, my mind wandered, think-ing about every possibility. I remember between crying fits pleading with God to take care of whatever was going on. I also remember calling my boss and trying to get the words out to tell him I wouldn't be in that day, but I was not coherent. I recall him saying, "It's ok. Do not worry about work. Take whatever time you need."

When I arrived, I trembled as I walked down the hall to his room. When he saw me, he mumbled some words that sounded like "Hello mom," but I could not make them out. I could tell by his eyes that he was trying to figure out who I was. It was as if I was a stranger to him.

I tried to remain calm and tell myself he was ok as I refused to believe we were headed towards another setback. I decided to talk to him about our visit the day prior, hoping this would stir up a conversation. With his continued blank stare, I knew he did not remember my visit. I tried to jar his memory and remind him that our good friends Curtis and Diana had visited, but he was adamant that he had not seen them as well.

Of course, my anxiety was going through the roof, and I could barely hold back the tears, wondering what had happened and how we had gotten to this point. It was the most disheartening thing I had ever seen. All I could think of was not only is he physically 'damaged,' but now his mind was going, and going fast. I prayed and prayed for the Lord to deliver him, but the answer I hoped for did not come swiftly. That day we sat mostly in silence as Gary slept most of the day away until I finally headed back home.

Less than 24 hours from my last visit, I received a call that Gary was struggling to comprehend what anyone was saying. Once again, I raced to the hospital as fast as my car would go. As I slowly walked into the room, I braced myself for the worst but was immediately comforted by the fact he called me by name. That peace was short-lived as he continued to talk, asking me over and over again why he was in the hospital. He was incessant about leaving and demanded an explanation of what was going on. I explained over and over, but it was as if I was talking to a young child.

Over the next several days, Gary's mind began to slip away, and his speech became more and more delayed. His tongue was swollen and covered with white foam. He was so unfocused and delirious that he could not follow any of the directions of his physical, occupational, or speech therapist. They tried on several occasions, but due to his mental condition, the choice was made to leave him in his bed and offer whatever services they could from his room.

It was so painful to watch all the progress that he had made go down the drain as his mental state deteriorated so badly that he began to yell and scream at people. He would shout random thoughts about the devil and the church. He would ask questions about if God had returned and if the pastors were still alive. He rambled constantly about the end of time and was adamant about the fact that evil things were happening all around him. He began to see things flying around the room and would ask me if I saw them, which of course, I never did. He would say that ants were crawling on him when there were none to be found. His face would twitch constantly, and his eyes expressed a sense of bewilderment and pain. Most nights, he laid in a trance state, rarely closing his eyes. He would stare at the ceiling, close his eyes for maybe five minutes, and then right back into the trance.

I could not believe what was happening, nor could I understand why again God would allow such a thing to happen. My husband had already been saved from physical death but was now dying a mental death. In fear of having my own mental breakdown, I made a difficult decision. A decision that some around me approved of, while others became frustrated. Nevertheless, I did not care what others thought. I had to save myself and my kids from losing both parents, so I left. I physically and mentally checked out. As I left the hospital that day, I questioned if I would ever come back because, in the depth of my soul, I wanted to leave this situation forever.

Whenever you fly, they tell you to put on your oxygen mask first before your kids so that you can be alive to help them. As insensitive as that may seem, I had to put on my oxygen mask and save myself. I was the glue holding the family together, and if I broke down, my kids would then be down two parents, and I could not allow that to happen. With the intent to keep me from a mental breakdown, I called Gary's sister Christine to be with him, and I escaped to a friend's house with my daughter to just relax and unwind. But I never got the chance. When I checked in on Gary, his situation was rapidly spiraling out of control. He cursed anyone and anything. He was so restless, constantly trying to get out of his bed to go fight this war that was playing in his mind.

One day, his mom came to visit, and while she was there, the unthinkable happened. He was having one of his fits, and as any mother would, went to comfort him. However, this triggered something in Gary, and he hit her across the face. Realizing what he had done sent him into a crying fit that lasted for quite some time. This made me even more fearful, and I called the pastors to go and anoint him, which they did.

My time away from the hospital was not peaceful. I could not take my mind off what Gary was going through. When I went back, I noticed he was calmer, yet his mind was still not clear. He continued to ramble about "the war," but then, out of nowhere, he looked me in the eye and said, "Pray for me. The devil is fighting to take me, but God is fighting harder."

I knew right then that he was not fighting a physical war but a spiritual battle with the devil. The enemy knew that Gary's testimony was bringing people closer to Christ, and that made Him so angry, he was ready to fight for Gary's life. He knew that the Lord had already given him victory over the grave, so he thought he would try another route and mess with his mind.

The word of God says in 1 Peter 5:8, "Stay Alert! Watch out for your great enemy, the devil. He prowls around like a roaring lion, looking for someone to devour." In this situation, the devil was roaring loudly and made it clear of his intention to steal my husband's mind and take him out once and for all. The stakes were just too high for him to let this miracle continue without a fight, and fight he did. Every step forward he made towards mental healing was met with an even harder blow. It almost appeared as if we had lost him mentally forever, BUT GOD!

After almost two weeks of a knockdown drag-out fight, the devil realized that he just did not have what it took to box with God and began to slowly lose his grip on Gary. Through the power of intercessory prayer and anointing by the elders, we kicked the devil's butt, and the final score yielded GOD 10- DEVIL -0. God prevailed, and as always, He wins! We could truly sing the song "Victory is Mine," as once again, the attempt to take Gary's life was halted. What a mighty God we serve!

Throughout this entire journey, the enemy continued to battle in our home. He let go of Gary, but in exchange, he began to attack our kids in ways that I will not share to protect them. But once again, through the power of prayer and anointing, my kids were protected from the enemy who was literally trying to destroy and take them from this earth. BUT GOD! Please do not get it twisted. The devil is strong, but MY GOD IS STRONGER!

I could not finish this book without sharing this incident, as the Bible has made it very clear that the devil is not sitting back, tiptoeing around, and sneaking into your life. NO! He is loud about it and makes it clear that he wants to take as many people as possible down and will do whatever it takes to steal, kill, and destroy. He is not ashamed about what he is doing as he knows that his time is short, and he will not stop at any cost. As children of God, we must use prayer and praise as our weapon to remove the devil out of every nook and cranny of our hearts, our minds, and our souls. We need to come at him just as strong as he comes after us and let him know HE WILL NOT WIN!

They say that the devil and his angels tremble when they hear the name Jesus so when he tries to come against you, shout, scream, yell His name! JESUS! JESUS! JESUS, and he has nothing else to do except flee. Victory is mine, declares the Lord. Receive your victory today, knowing that God's roar is louder, and He will defeat the devil every time. So, devil... GET TO STEPPING!

# Scriptures for Reflection

## Ephesians 6:10-11
"A final word: Be strong in the Lord and in his mighty power. Put on all of God's armor so that you will be able to stand firm against all strategies of the devil."

## 2 Thessalonians 3:3
"But the Lord is faithful; he will strengthen you and guard you from the evil one."

CHAPTER 11

# Faith Finale

It has been almost two years since my husband's surgery, and we have experienced a plethora of emotions. Although he has very little mobility from the waist down, he is doing well and is making progress. We give God praise daily for sparing his life and literally taking him from his death bed. Together we are navigating this new life and are hopeful that one day God will allow him to walk again. We have learned many lessons in this journey, but most importantly, to have to trust God and surrender our lives to Him fully. I have learned that James 1:2 which says, "Dear brothers and sisters, when troubles of any kind come your way, consider it an opportunity for great joy," is truly a guide to living.

Although I did not see it at the time, I now can say that my trials have given me the best gift, and that is the gift of salvation. Through this trial, I not only was able to see and experience a modern-day miracle but my life was changed for the better. My love for the Father grew exponentially.

It may be hard to believe, but through it all, I realized that God must love me a lot to provide me with an experience that would literally save my soul. Not only did He save me, but he also used my story for His Glory and led many others to kneel at the foot of the cross and give their lives to Christ. If my pain allows God to be magnified, then it is all worth it.

It has not been easy, but I have chosen to no longer live in self-pity or doubt but embrace every step of this journey and trust in the God that I know is with me every step of the way. Like Jonah in the Bible, there were many times where I wanted to run far, far away and hide from my situation, my family, and perhaps even God. But I learned that being broken to the core can lead you to the foot of the cross and ultimately lead you to the most precious gift: Jesus Christ.

Today, I challenge each reader to turn their trials into joy and embrace our Father. He is waiting with arms open wide to soothe all your pains and love you beyond what you could ever imagine. One day Christ will return, and your journey right now is preparing you for that glorious day. Choose faith over fear. Try Him. Trust Him with full surrender. Nothing less. Christ never fails! It is okay to be shattered by God's design.

*Tributes*

# A Daughter's Journey

Since the moment my dad went into surgery my life changed completely. It was a couple of days before my first day of 7th grade and my dad was going to have surgery on his spine. Right before he was taken into the operating room we went in and said goodbye and prayed with him. I wasn't nervous because we were surrounded by many friends and family members who were in the waiting room to be with us. We played games and told jokes to help pass the time which turned out to be 10 hours. Finally, the doctor came out and pulled my mom aside and let her know how the surgery went. My Mom shared that my dad had come through the surgery and was recovering. I was ecstatic that my dad was ok and I could now focus on starting my first day of school. I was confident all would be well and dad would be home soon.

Things did not go as I thought and we spent the next 5 months in 2 different hospitals where I spent a lot of time often doing my homework. It was a tough time, but luckily I had my best friend Paris to help me get through it. I was happy when we finally got to bring my dad home. Although he was home, I began to make some very poor choices and times became very hard for me. I had a lot of ups and downs dealing with our family situation. I became aggressive to kids at school and had bad relationships with my teachers. To top it off I got into mess with this boy that I learned never really cared about me. During that time I thought I had to be extra tough and be an adult because my mom needed me, but I realized I was not ready to take that on, and slowly I started just being a regular teen again.

Two years later, I am relieved that we made it through that tough time and I am looking forward to a bright future in high school. Through this time some people asked me if I still believe in God? The truthful answer is I am not sure yet, but I can't wait to find out and experience Him for myself. I am beyond ready to see what is in store for me.


Taylor Willis
*Daughter*

# Messages of Gratitude
## from Cassandra and Gary

O ur hearts remain overwhelmed with the love and support we have experienced throughout our journey. Thank you to all of our friends and family who visited at our toughest times, spent the night in the hospital so Gary wouldn't be alone, sent us meals, installed accessible flooring, provided financial blessing, took care of our children, gave us hugs when we were breaking, but most importantly prayed for us and stood by us through it all. We can never repay you for being our village.

**We want to give a big thanks to our parents,** who showed us more love than we ever could have expected. First to our mother, Loretta Hunter. Thank you for pushing through your own pain of seeing your son at death's door and continuing to be there for us. Your faith is remarkable, and we are grateful for how God blessed us with you. To our Father, Roland Hunter. Thank you for being our quiet soldier who supported us and kept us encouraged during the tough days of rehab. You are truly a man of God. To our parents Joe and Adelaide Hendrix. The sacrifice you made making multiple trips to be by our side, help with the kids, cook meals, and be a shoulder to cry on will never be forgotten. You have encouraged us and always reminded us that God always prevails. You always have and will always be our true superheroes.

**To our siblings Valerie, Raymond, Aaron, Christine, Michael, Leilani, Evan, Harold, and Tracy.** There was never a time where we felt alone in this journey, and this is all because of you. Your ongoing love and never wavering support for us go beyond what we could have ever imagined. You made sure we were taken care of every step of the way and always took care of us and the kids. Words cannot express the love we have for you. We can truly say we have the best siblings ever!

**To our neurosurgeon Dr. Vartan Tashjian.** You were not just our surgeon but became part of our family. You are not only a dedicated doctor but just a caring soul whose bedside manner is beyond what any patient could ever imagine. You were heaven-sent, and the compassion you showed us will never be forgotten. Thank you for never giving up!

**To our pastors, Dr. Keith Ainsworth Morris, Dr. Jerrold Thompson, and Dr. Andrea King.** Your love and nurture of our family during this difficult time went beyond what we could have ever hoped for. You restored our faith in pastoral care, and we will never be able to repay you for what you did and still do for our family. We love you!

**And finally, to our work family.** We are forever grateful for the love and support shown to us by the staff of the Corona Norco Unified School District and La Sierra University. You all showed what it means to go above and beyond to help a colleague. Thank you!

# *To My Original Sista Circle from Cassandra*

**Valerie Middleton** – My "sister-in-love." You planned to stay a few days but ended up staying a month. You will never know how much comfort you brought me, knowing that Gary was not alone, and I could just breathe and take a break from the hospital. Thank you!

**Christine Davis** – Watching your brother in such a terrible state took its toll on you, but somehow you never gave up and continued to be there for the kids and me. Your encouragement and listening ear made my toughest days bearable. Thank you for always having my back and being an awesome sister in love.

**Lisa Hayes** – You have proven that distance never can take away a person's love for each other. It had been years since we had seen each other, yet you stepped in and brought me so much encouragement. You took time out of your schedule to love on my babies, cook the food that they still talk about today, and simply hold my hand. I can still hear you say, "Whatever you need. I got you." You lived up to those words and blessed me beyond what I could have ever imagined.

**Kammie Thomaseec** – Every week you gave up your weekend to travel eight hours to be with me. You will never know how much I appreciated you standing by my side and being a constant place for me to cry, vent, and fall apart. You were my rock, and I am forever grateful. You held me when I was too weak to stand and encouraged me when I gave up hope. You still, to this day, have shown me the true meaning of family. Blood made of cousins, but love made us sisters.

**Leilani Kim Stamper** – My big sister and best friend. You have cried with me, held me, screamed with me, and prayed with me. It did not matter if it was 12 noon or 2:00 a.m. I knew that you would answer the phone and get me through whatever was going on. When I felt hopeless and wanted to succumb to doubt and could not pray, you flooded the heavens on my behalf and gave me the words that I needed to make it one more day. Thank you for traveling multiple times to be with me and give me the strength I needed to keep moving on. You never wavered in your belief that Gary would make it, and your faith made my faith even stronger. You have been my rock, and I love you more than words can express. God knew that I would go through this time, and in His infinite wisdom, He chose you to be my sister, and for that, I am forever grateful. I love you to infinity and beyond.

# About the Author

Cassandra Willis is an educator who currently serves as Director of Student and Family Support Services for a local school district. As an educational leader, she has dedicated her life to supporting children and helping them reach their potential academically, spiritually, and socially. She has received numerous awards in the area of education, including Principal of the Year, The Valuing Diversity Award given by the Association of California School Administrators, and District Administrator of the Year.

She has a passion for working with young people and has led out in children's and youth ministries for 20 years. Most importantly, she is a woman of faith who enjoys nothing more than spending time with her husband of 26 years, Gary, and their children Gary Jr. and Taylor.

CPSIA information can be obtained
at www.ICGtesting.com
Printed in the USA
FSHW021713250621
82635FS

9 781948 877782